Dogs Dogs Dogs

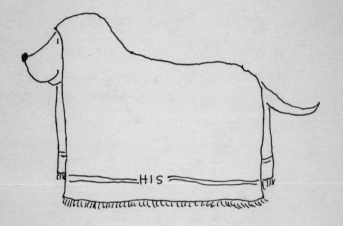

HIS

Their care and training

written and illustrated by Carol Benjamin

Watermill Press
Mahwah, N.J.

*For Mimi Kahn, my sibling, inventor of the
midnight gongs, and all-around swell person*

Contents of this edition copyright © 1981 by Watermill Press,
Mahwah, New Jersey

Printed in the United States of America

ISBN   0-89375-458-7

Contents

1

A Puppy
of Your Own

Sometimes the only friend who will do is your dog. He won't tire on long walks. He's the perfect companion when you want to be alone. He lends an ear for secrets, yet he'll never tell. He's ready to have a good time any time you are, but he's patient when you are busy or not in the mood to play. (Well, most of the time, anyway.)

A dog is simple, open, and loving. He is as delightful as the first spring day, as wonderful as an ice-cream cone (double dip, of course), as surprising as the last snow of the season. It's great fun to have a dog of your own.

Bed and Board

Your new puppy will need a corner all his own where he can sleep, chew on a dog toy, or just feel secure and private. There's no need to spend lots of money on a dog bed or a mattress for your puppy. Make him a beautiful bed out of a cardboard box. Be sure to cut the front low enough for him to get in and out. An old towel or soft cloth on the bottom of the box will make his bed a cozy spot. Decorate the outside of the box with your favorite drawings and your puppy's name. The puppy in this book has a name, too. His name is Jelly Bean!

If Jelly should have an "accident" in his bed, wash the towel, and decorate a fresh box. Keeping Jelly's bed clean is very important and will help teach him to keep himself and your house clean.

Until Jelly is five or six months old, he should eat three times a day. After that, he can get along well on two meals a day, one in the morning and one in the evening. Small and medium-sized dogs eat one meal a day, starting when they are one year old. Large and extra-large dogs should stay with two meals a day.

Jelly can eat dry dog food mixed with some canned dog food or with cottage cheese, cooked eggs, or leftover meat and vegetables. He needs lots of fresh, cool water to drink, especially in hot weather. If you feed Jelly at regular times and limit his snacking, you'll never have a picky eater to worry about. Most dogs like dog food and gobble it down with lots of enthusiasm.

A Visit to the Dog Doctor

When you first get Jelly Bean, he'll have to go to the veterinarian for a checkup and shots. The shots protect him against the diseases of rabies, distemper, hepatitis, and leptospirosis. Most dogs take their shots without any fuss at all. The vet will check Jelly Bean over and make sure that he is healthy. He may tell you how much to feed him and what kind of food would be best. He can also show you how to trim Jelly's nails and keep his ears clean. A trip to the vet is exciting and scary for a little puppy, but, as you can see, it is very important. Jelly will probably take a long nap when he gets home. By the time he wakes up, he will have forgotten all about his shots and checkup and be ready to play.

Neatness Counts

If you brush Jelly's coat every day and keep it shining and clean, people will enjoy petting him more. Jelly will like that. And while *he* doesn't care what he looks like and *he* wouldn't mind running through mud puddles all day long, your mom and dad will like him better if he's relatively clean, at least for a dog.

Grooming time is special for another reason. It's a very quiet, private moment for you and you alone to share with your dog. It's the time to tell him a story, sing to him, tell him all your troubles. A dog is always a good listener. He never snitches. He never makes fun. He hardly ever gets bored.

Jelly won't need a bath very often. When he does need one, you can get him clean in no time with this funny, easy method.

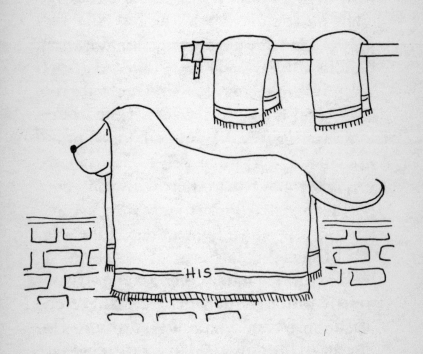

HIS

Don't fill the tub with water. Put Jelly Bean in the bathtub. Run some warm water and, using a spray attachment or a plastic container, wet Jelly's coat. Next, soap Jelly up with dog shampoo or baby shampoo. Rub the soap in everywhere, except Jelly's head. Wash his head carefully with a washcloth and plain water. When you are finished, run the water again and rinse Jelly until he's squeaky clean. It's very important to get all the soap out of his coat.

When the rinse is over, toss a big towel over Jelly, right in the tub, and rub, rub, rub until he's about half dry. Then let him out, let him shake, let him run around indoors. When he's all dry, give him a good brushing and watch him shine.

Keeping Your Puppy Fit

Every dog needs some exercise. If your pup is little, he may get a lot of exercise dashing around the house. Medium-sized dogs and big dogs need to get their exercise

out-of-doors. Encourage Jelly to run and play by throwing a ball or a stick for him to fetch. Run around with him. Let him play with another friendly dog. Even though Jelly Bean loves you best, he still needs to play with other people and with other dogs, too.

Do Not Disturb

Every dog needs some rest. A young puppy gets tired very quickly. When he's asleep, you don't have to tiptoe or whisper. But you shouldn't wake him until he's ready to get up all by himself. Then he'll be full of pep and ready to play with you.

A puppy must learn to be by himself sometimes even when he's not sleeping and even when he doesn't want to be by himself. Part of growing up to be a good member of your family means that he must not fuss and cry when no one can play with him. He must not whine in the middle of the night.

He has to learn, as we all do, that sometimes he will have to entertain himself. He should always have a dog bone or a toy to chew. Chewing can keep a dog busy for hours. Perhaps there's a cat in the family who might like to play with him or keep him company. He might enjoy being out on the terrace or in the yard where he can sniff interesting smells blowing in on the breezes. He might enjoy seeing children play or watching the dog next door. But he cannot be entertained all the time. He must learn to be quiet when his family is busy with other things. A spoiled dog is no fun.

If your puppy cries when you leave him alone, first make sure he's OK. See that he has water. Make sure he's had his walk. Give him something to chew. If he still whines, tell him NO, NO, NO. Don't go in and cuddle him or he'll continue to cry and cry for attention. Little by little, he'll learn to rest and play quietly. He'll understand that when you go to school, soon you will

JELLY BEAN

be home to play with him again. A nice romp with you in the morning will help make the wait easier. Then you can both look forward to seeing each other later in the day.

2

A Lot to Learn

When you first get your puppy, he has already learned a lot of things from his mother and from his brothers and sisters. He has learned some important manners. His mother may have taught him not to nip too hard. She probably taught him not to stray too far away. He has also probably learned to size up the other pups, to see which ones were the strongest and where he fit into the picture. Now that your puppy is in a human family, you have to teach him

things that will help him to be a good family member.

All dogs have some human rules to learn. They cannot get up on the dining-room table and walk through the mashed potatoes. They cannot relieve themselves on the living-room rug. They cannot eat the roast beef, lick the butter, put their paws in the green peas, or go poking around in the garbage looking for goodies. They mustn't cry when left alone, nor bark in the middle of the night. When you ask them to do something, such as SIT or LIE DOWN, they should do it right away.

The best way to tell your puppy what you like and what you don't like is to teach him the words NO and OK. When you sternly tell your puppy NO, he will know he's doing something he shouldn't. When you hand him a dog treat and tell him OK, he'll know that it's OK for him to take the treat. When he makes the right choice, tell him GOOD BOY. When he breaks the rules, tell him BAD DOG, NO, SHAME! Pretty soon he'll cut out most of the bad behavior and be an easy dog to live with. He *does* want to please you. But he'll never be perfect. Who is?

HOUSEBREAKING YOUR PUPPY

Housebreaking is easy and will make perfect sense to you if you think about the behavior of many wild animals. The wolf, a close relative of the dog, is a den animal. That means that the young pups are raised in a den for their safety and protection. If the den were to get dirty, the small puppies would get sick and they would not survive. So the habit of keeping the den clean is connected to the very survival of the species. When the pups are still small, they toddle out of the den to relieve themselves and then rush back in for safety. As they get older, they relieve themselves further away from the den and stay out longer to play.

If you keep your puppy in a small area, such as a blocked-off section of the kitchen for the first few weeks that you have him, and if you walk him regularly, he will housebreak himself very quickly. He will not want to soil an area where he must sleep. So, if you schedule his walks carefully, he will wait for you to take him out before relieving himself. Housebreaking is really that simple.

Housebreaking Schedule

Here is a good schedule for a young puppy:

Before school:	Walk puppy Feed puppy Walk puppy 20 minutes play
Lunch time:	Walk puppy Feed puppy Walk puppy 20 minutes play
After school:	Walk puppy 20 minutes play
Before dinner:	Feed puppy Walk puppy 20 minutes play
Before bedtime:	Walk puppy Put puppy to bed for the night.

As your puppy gets trained, you can cut down on his walks, one at a time. By the time he's one year old, three walks a day will be enough.

This schedule is set up so that you can take care of your puppy by yourself. Of course, if your parents can help, that will make it easier for you. Then the puppy's last walk can be at *their* bedtime. As long as the puppy gets to go out on time, he will learn to wait. As he begins to know where he can and can't relieve himself, you can let him play for a longer time. Soon, he will be able to have the run of the entire kitchen between walks. When this happens, you can begin to take him into the rest of the house for a few minutes at a time. Once he is reliable about housebreaking, and you know he won't chew the furniture, he can have the run of the house. Now it is time to teach him some other things. Puppies love to learn.

OBEDIENCE TRAINING

Week One: Teaching Your Puppy to Sit

1   Tell Jelly Bean SIT. If he doesn't sit, gently pull up on his collar as you push down on his rump.

2   Practice this a few times a day until Jelly will sit when you say SIT. Break Jelly by saying OK. Each time he sits after you say SIT, praise him by petting him and saying GOOD BOY.

3   After the first few days, work outside with Jelly on the SIT. There are more distractions outside and it will be harder to make him sit. But every dog must learn to obey inside his home as well as out-of-doors. You never know where you'll be when Jelly's training will be needed! Always praise him for good work and play with him when the work is over.

Week Two: Teaching Your Puppy to Stay

1   Put Jelly on a SIT. Use the leash for
this command. Now tell him STAAAY,
and slowly swing a flat, open hand
towards his nose. Hand signals are very

important. Dogs are better at watching than they are at listening.

2   As you give the command, back away to the end of the leash. After a minute, break Jelly by saying OK. When he wiggles up to you, pleased with his

work, praise him warmly. Now, *find a new spot,* and practice again.

3 STAY is a very important command and will take a lot of practice. As you work with Jelly Bean, make the *stays* longer and longer, surprising him every now and then with a nice, short one. Each time you say SIT, STAY, and he waits for your OK to break, tell him GOOD BOY, JELLY. I LOVE YOU!

Week Three: Teaching Your Puppy to Heel

1 Jelly is going to learn to walk properly on a leash. The command HEEL means that he will walk on your *left* side, his head even with your hip, and at the same speed that you walk. If you tell him HEEL, he cannot dash ahead to play with another dog. He cannot

lag behind to sniff every tree. Before you give him the command HEEL, let him sniff around and relieve himself. Then he'll be able to pay attention during his lesson.

First have Jelly *sit* and *stay* at your left side. Tell him HEEL and begin to walk forward *even if he just sits there looking silly.* Pat your left leg, whistle if you can, and cheer him on. COME ON, JELLY! LET'S HEEL. If you have to, tug a little at the leash and get Jelly moving along with you. As he comes along at your side, talk to him, pat your leg, remind him to HEEL, tug the leash if he strays off, and tell him GOOD BOY when he trots along at your side! Whew! Heeling is a lot of work. Be gentle. It will take Jelly a few weeks to heel really well.

2 When you stop walking, Jelly Bean is supposed to sit *automatically.* That is why you taught him to sit before you

began teaching him to heel. It will take a couple of weeks of practice for him to do the automatic sit automatically. In the beginning, when you stop, you will say JELLY, SIT. He will—and you will pet him and say GOOD DOG, JELLY BEAN! Then you will say HEEL, and begin walking again. Practice every day, rain or shine, outside. Soon Jelly will walk at your side when you say HEEL and he'll sit neatly at your side when you stop walking. Always praise him *after* he sits.

3   A dog is called a puppy until he is one year old. Your little puppy, at three months old, can learn to *sit* and *stay*. Your big puppy, at five or six months old, can learn to *heel*. But what about older dogs? Your Jelly Bean might be seven years old. Can he still learn? You bet! An old dog can learn new tricks, new games, new commands—and he'll

love every minute of it. With all dogs,
young and old, heeling will take a lot
of outdoor practice, a lot of patience,
and a heap of praise.

*Week Four: Teaching Your Puppy
to Come*

1 This week, you can begin the important, easy command, COME. You
   will still be working hard on HEEL.
   You will still be practicing SIT and
   STAY. Just add each new command to
   your daily practice with Jelly Bean.

   Put Jelly on a SIT STAY. Go to the end
   of the leash and turn around to face
   him. Wait a short while. Now call him
   to come to you, saying JELLY BEAN,
   COME! Bend down. Clap your hands.
   Whistle. Get that dog! And when you
   get him, praise him, hug him, kiss
   him—and do it all again and again and

again. Soon Jelly will come whenever
you call him. Work on-leash outside,
off-leash inside, and off-leash outside *if*
your yard is fenced. Above all, keep
that Jelly Bean safe. Don't let him run
around loose and get lost or hurt.

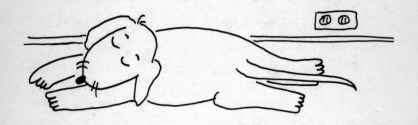

Week Five: Teaching Your Puppy to Lie Down

1   Teach the DOWN *after* an outing so that Jelly is tired and wants to lie down anyway. Once he knows the command, he'll lie down any time you tell him to.

Put Jelly Bean on a SIT STAY. Pat the floor and say DOWN. Now gently draw Jelly's legs forward so that he is lying down. Let him roll over if he wants to and rub his belly. That will make him *love* to lie down on command. Speak firmly and quietly to him. Keep calm. This command can be very hard for the first few days, but it is very important—and, once Jelly knows it, he won't mind it at all.

Week Six: Stay in the House

Jelly Bean's safety is in your hands. Some people think their dogs are "car smart" and can run around loose all day without getting into big trouble. Dogs just don't have the brain power to understand automobiles. Your dog should be with *you*, on-leash, when you and he are out-of-doors. Or, you can play with him without a leash if your yard is fenced. But even with the best of intentions on your part, your dog may sneak out of the house and run free. Once he gets into this bad habit, it is hard to break him of it. But it is not impossible. Here's how you can do it.

Jelly knows the word STAY. You have taught him SIT and STAY and LIE DOWN and STAY. When doing these commands, STAY means *freeze*. Jelly Bean is supposed to "glue" himself to the spot where you gave him the command. Now he will learn that STAY also means *stick around*.

1   For one week, tell Jelly OK whenever you take him for a walk. Say OK just as you and he step out of the house. You can start doing this while he is learning LIE DOWN. It is very easy. However, in order for Jelly to learn this safety command, everyone who walks him will have to help. Any time anyone takes him out for a stroll, they must tell him OK just as they are stepping out the door. That should be followed by GOOD BOY, JELLY.

2 After a week of telling Jelly OK before
he leaves the house, put him on-leash,
walk up to the door, and brace yourself.
Now, open the door—but don't say a
word. If Jelly Bean lunges forward,
pull back hard on the leash and tell
him NO, STAY IN THE HOUSE. *Do
not* make him sit and stay, or lie down
and stay, or do anything else. He can
move around. He can stand up. He can
lean on the wall. He can beg, plead,
drool, and cry to go out. Once he waits,
tell him OK and take him for a walk,
praising him for going out the door
after hearing the OK command, and
not before.

3 Every time you walk Jelly (or anyone
else does), tell him OK as you leave the
house with him. Once in a while, don't
say anything. If he starts to dart out,
jerk back on the leash and say NO!
STAY IN THE HOUSE. When you
are leaving without him, tell him NO,

JELLY BEAN, YOU HAVE TO STAY IN THE HOUSE. You'll be surprised at how fast he will understand exactly what you are saying.

Once Jelly is reliable, he won't run out the door when you are coming in with your arms full of school books. He'll be a lot safer than if he continued to slip out every time someone opened the door. If you reinforce the training by praising him every time he does the right thing, you will have a trained, safe, and happy dog.

3

Fun and Games

Write Your Dog a Letter

What happens when you go to camp or go away on vacation for a week or two? You'll miss Jelly Bean, and he'll miss you. Why not write him a letter?

Of course, Jelly Bean can't read! But you can "write" him a scent letter. A dog's nose is terrific when it comes to getting information from odors. Take a small piece of cloth. Rub your hands on it for a few minutes. Put the cloth in a plastic

sandwich bag, and seal it with masking tape. Now you can address an envelope to Jelly Bean, and seal your "letter" into the envelope.

When someone opens Jelly's "letter" for him, and holds open the plastic bag so that he can smell the cloth, he'll think of you. Your dog will love to get scent letters from you whenever you are away. Keeping in touch can be lots of fun!

A Hobo Hike for Two

Pack some dog biscuits, a sandwich, a jar of cold water (ice cubes will keep the water cool on a hot day), a ball, and a dime (in case you have to make a phone call). Take Jelly on his leash and, with your hobo pack, go exploring with your dog pal.

You can go exploring on your own block. Look for oddly shaped rocks. See how many kinds of trees there are. Try out Jelly's training. Hike in a park. Stop for

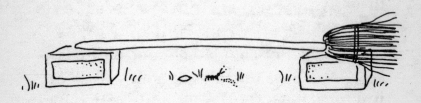

your picnic. Play ball. Perhaps Jelly Bean will fetch the ball for you—or swim after it.

You can hike with Jelly on a trail or on a shopping street. Now that you have trained Jelly Bean, he can even go inside many stores with you. It's fun to shop, hike, picnic, and explore with a dog of your own.

Jump Over a Broom

Dogs love to be active. They love to learn. They love to perform. You can combine all these things, as well as your dog's love for food, into one great trick.

Borrow a broom, or just an old broomstick, and lay it across two bricks so that it is just a few inches off the ground. Take Jelly Bean, on-leash, and run towards the broomstick with him. When you get to it, say JUMP, JELLY, and jump over the broomstick with Jelly Bean. Keep running and jumping over the broom, back and forth, until you are both used to it and feeling good and silly. Now you can play with Jelly and give him a treat.

Practice every day, for a few minutes at a time, until Jelly loves to jump over the broom. You can now start trying to get him to jump over the broom without you, by running him up to it and saying JUMP, JELLY.

When Jelly is a good jumper, willing to go over the broom with you *and* without you, raise the broom, a tiny bit at a time. First, turn the bricks on their sides for a higher jump. Next, balance the broomstick on two paint cans. If Jelly is a big dog, one day he'll be able to jump the broomstick when it is balanced on two chairs. If he's small, the paint cans will be a good, high jump for him.

Any healthy dog can learn to jump over a broomstick. It's great fun, good exercise, and a good trick for showing off with your pal, Jelly Bean.

Collections Can Be Fun

You may collect stamps, baseball cards, shells, miniatures, coins, or fossils. Why not start a collection based on your love of dogs?

You can start a collection of dog miniatures. You can find some in toy stores for very little money. If you get rich one day, you can add miniature bronzes and carved wooden dogs to your collection. If anyone you know is traveling, ask for a small dog statue from a foreign country.

Some kids collect dog licenses. If you can begin to gather them from all over the country, little by little, you will have some wonderful shapes, and lots of odd names of towns in your collection. The tags will look terrific mounted on a board or pinned onto your bulletin board and hung up in your room. You can even make a collection out of rabies tags! Every year, when the dog gets his new tag, the old ones are thrown away.

Ask your neighbors and friends to save them for your collection. Some are colored. Some are shaped like bones or hearts. They can be fun to collect.

Puppets and toys modeled after dogs are also good to collect. You can find modern toys in any toy store, and antique ones in antique shops and junk shops—maybe even up in someone's attic. You will enjoy playing with them and displaying them. And, over the years, some will get more and more valuable.

Dog books are fun to collect, too. This one can be the beginning of your own dog-book library. There are many books with stories about dogs and many others which tell you facts about dogs: how they live in the wild, how to train them, how different breeds came to be. You will enjoy reading your dog books again and again.

You can look for dogs on anything—stamps, coins, bookends, doorstops, cartoons from magazines, or patches to sew on your jeans. Make the collection that will be the most fun for you. You can collect things to display, wear, play with, read, enjoy. Collecting can be lots of fun.

Fetch a Stick

Active play is great fun for dogs. They enjoy dashing about, carrying things in their mouths, pretending to come up to you with their prize, and then dashing away. Jelly Bean is no exception.

Play with a stick. Act as if it is the most interesting stick in the world. Soon Jelly Bean will want it. Now tease him with it for just a second. DO YOU WANT THIS STICK, JELLY? GO FETCH. And toss the stick as far as you can. Jelly will run for the stick and run around with it. He may toss it in the air a little and catch it. He may chew it to smithereens. No matter. Sticks are cheap.

Call Jelly in a cheerful way, bending down on one knee and clapping your hands. HERE, JELLY. COME. GOOD

BOY, JELLY. If he comes to you, *don't take the stick*. He mustn't feel you'll always steal his treasure. Pet him and then let him run off with the stick. Now call again. This time, grasp the stick and say OUT. This time, throw the stick immediately for Jelly to fetch. Now Jelly will trust you and like the game better. As you play with him, sometimes take the stick, and sometimes let Jelly keep it, chew it, hide it, drop it, bury it, sit on it, do whatever *he* likes with it. Sometimes, take the stick and toss it for Jelly. You will know when he wants to keep it, and when he wants to play fetch with it. Soon enough, he'll *give* you the stick when he wants to fetch. Soon enough, he'll *find* a stick all by himself and bring it to you to begin this game.

Find the Glove

Do you remember when you lost your left glove? Now you will have a use for the *right* glove.

Go out in the yard or the park with Jelly,
and show him the glove. Let him sniff it.
Now put him on a SIT STAY and put the
glove down *where he can see it*. Tell him
JELLY, FIND THE GLOVE. OK. FIND
THE GLOVE. Just out of curiosity, he
should go over to the glove. At this point,
praise him, and try to get him to pick it up.
If he does, pet him, and give him a treat.

Hide the glove again, still within Jelly's
sight. Keep this up for a whole week,
playing inside the house as well as outside.
Once Jelly is enthusiastic about retrieving
the glove, begin to hide it a little farther
away. Don't make it too hard for Jelly. He
must always find the glove within a couple
of minutes or he'll get bored and quit. If
you hide the glove under a chair and he
can't find it, help him out. Walk near the
chair and say GOOD BOY. FIND IT.
FIND THE GLOVE. Keep encouraging
Jelly to use his nose and find the glove.
Pretty soon you'll be able to hide it in

another room, on the bed, behind a tree, on the steps, almost anywhere at all. Jelly will love to search with his nose and your family will love this game. It's very entertaining.

Photograph Your Dog

You don't have to be a great photographer to take a great dog picture. Luckily, you have a great model—Jelly Bean.

If you are a brand-new photographer, it will be easier for you to take good shots of Jelly when he is still. You can use fast film and shoot your pictures without flash. Begin indoors, where Jelly will be calmer and easier to control. Open the curtains and let the sun shine in. Flash can be handy in providing light when there isn't enough, but it tends to make a dog's eyes look spooky. So place Jelly where the natural light is the best, and put him on a SIT STAY or a DOWN STAY. This will give

you all the time you need to focus and get ready to shoot. Your trained dog will stay put while you take his pictures. That's just one fringe benefit of training.

If you have another pet, the two together will make a terrific picture. They're bound to lick each other, lean on each other, play a game, or have a make-believe fight. That should make for a really good shot.

Once you get used to photographing your dog when he's indoors and still, let him move about, and try for good action shots. When photographing a moving object, you will need more speed. That means you'll need more light. Now's the time to move outdoors. There you will be able to get good pictures, with a great variety of backdrops.

Photographing your dog can be fun. You'll even begin to see different things about him when you look at him through the camera lens. You may start to notice the texture of his coat, the gleam you want to catch in his eyes, the shine on his nose, even his best profile! If you take your time, you can get wonderful shots of your dog just being a dog.

Join a Kennel Club

If you love dogs and just can't get enough of them, you might enjoy joining your local Kennel Club. There are Kennel Clubs all over. If your vet can't help you find one, write to:

> The American Kennel Club
> 51 Madison Avenue
> New York, New York 10010

They can send you a list of Kennel Clubs all over the United States.

The Clubs put on dog shows and always need members to help take tickets, serve refreshments, run errands, clean up after the dogs, and make announcements. Clubs meet once a month and show films about dogs, have interesting guest speakers, and breaks for milk and doughnuts.

Take Your Dog to School

There are two ways to take Jelly Bean to school. You can take him to a dog school, one where dogs· and owners attend class together, and work on the basic commands. This is a fun and social way to train a dog. He will learn to obey you with other dogs around. He may do so well that he wins a trophy at graduation.

Perhaps you will train Jelly all by yourself, following the instructions in this book. Then you may be able to get permission from your teacher to take Jelly Bean to *your* school. You can give a talk and demonstration on dog training! Jelly Bean can show off how well he can heel, sit, lie down, stay, and come—all on command from you, his dog trainer.

You can have Jelly fetch a ball, sniff, and

find a glove. The other kids will love your show. If your teacher agrees that this would be an enjoyable project, she may get you permission to bring Jelly in for a day or for half a day. Jelly will love school. The kids will clap for him, and when your talk is over, they can pet him. He'll feel happy and excited, and you'll be *so* proud of him. That Jelly Bean—he's a great dog!

4

Ask the Dog Trainer

(Questions and answers that will help you understand your dog even better.)

When my dog Spaghetti meets another dog on the street, he rolls over onto his back. Why does he do that?

Spaghetti is "talking" in dog-body-language to the other dog. He is showing that he is willing to be submissive, or obedient. Perhaps the other dog is bigger or older. After Spaghetti rolls over, the other dog won't feel "up tight" and then they can play.

When I come home from school, my Golden Retriever, Fanny, meets me at the door with a toy in her mouth. Then she "talks" with the toy still in her mouth. Is she acting silly on purpose?

Some dogs do "crack jokes" and act silly just to get a laugh. But your pup is a Retriever and whenever she gets really excited, she acts out her instincts—she retrieves. When you come home, she is so happy to see you that she is beside herself! Retrieving her toy helps her to greet you without going totally bananas.

Whenever I bring my dog Red home, and I'm unlocking the door, he rolls on the ground and rubs himself all over the walls right outside the apartment door. Does this mean something special?

Red is leaving his scent outside the entrance to his home. This way, if other dogs pass your door, they will know that that is the beginning of Red's property. Rubbing and rolling also feel good to your dog and he may rub and roll on carpets and grass as well.

Why do dogs chase their tails?

Dogs chase their tails for the same reason that babies play with their toes. It's fun.

When I tell my dog Mimi to SIT and STAY, she sits and then she lies down. Why does she do this? She is a very good dog. Should I just let her lie down?

Mimi is a very smart dog. She has figured out what STAY means, and has determined that if she's going to be stuck in one spot, she might as well get comfortable. While that seems pretty reasonable, it spoils her training. Actually, by lying down, Mimi is breaking the SIT command. So, when she lies down on a SIT, pull her up by her collar and repeat SIT, STAY in a firm voice. A well-trained dog will obey the command *as given*.

Do dogs like to watch other dogs on TV?

Most dogs don't enjoy watching TV because it has no scent. Sometimes a young puppy will look at the TV and then walk up to it and sniff it. Once the pup finds out that the dogs don't smell like dogs, he tends to ignore the television from then on. Of course, there *are* exceptions. Some dogs and many cats do like television, particularly shows with lots of action.

My dog Michael goes into the garbage and has a feast every time he's left alone in the kitchen. How can I teach him not to do this?

The best way to stop a dog from stealing garbage is the easiest way. Either put the can behind closed doors under the sink, or buy a can with a lid.

Which are faster runners, male dogs or female dogs?

Statistics show that, among racing greyhounds, the males are faster in short races, and the females win more of the longer races. Speed depends a lot on the breed you have. Some dogs were bred to run, and run fast. Others are slower but have other talents, such as retrieving or guarding.

My aunt says that poodles are the silliest dogs. What do you think?

Poodles are known for clowning around. It can be a lot of fun to watch them show off. Terriers are very energetic and like to fool around in front of an audience, too. My Golden Retriever often makes me laugh. But the funniest dog I ever saw was a miniature Dachshund named Balzac who used to beg for food by bringing *his* dish to the table when people were eating. If they were foolish enough not to fill his dish with tidbits, he'd pick it up again and bang it into their legs. Fortunately, he was very small, and so was his dish.

What's a great treat for my dog when it's his birthday or when I just feel like giving him a good time?

For any healthy dog, a nice hike to a new place would be a terrific treat. Don't make your dog HEEL, except when crossing the street or walking where it is very crowded.

Let him sniff and pull and explore. Show him a new street, a new park, a duck pond, where he can wet his nose and his toes. Dogs love to explore—to see and smell new places, to meet new people, to find a dog pal, and run and play. A hike would be a great birthday present for your dog, any day of the year.

Dogs, dogs, dogs! They have fun doing just about anything you like to do. Any time you can let Jelly Bean in on your fun, you'll make him a really happy dog. And, any time you let Jelly Bean in on your fun, he'll make *you* a really happy kid. Give your dog just a little, and he'll give you back everything he's got! Life is always sweeter when you have a dog to love.